THE

It is asked:
"What is sweeter than mead?"
And the answer runs:
    "The dew of heaven."
"And what is sweeter than dew?"
    "Honey from Hybla."
"And what is sweeter than honey?"
    "Nectar."
"And sweeter still?"
    "A kiss."
Latin epigram

KISS

Maryam Sachs

CollinsPublishersSanFrancisco

A Division of HarperCollins*Publishers*

First published in USA 1992 by
Collins Publishers San Francisco

Copyright © 1991 Wilhelm Heyne Verlag GmbH & Co.
All rights reserved, including the right of reproduction in whole
or in part in any form.

Library of Congress Cataloging-in-Publication Data
The Kiss: poetic pictures and texts/collected and selected
by Maryam Sachs.
p.   cm.
Translation of: Der Kuss
Includes bibliographical references.
ISBN 0-00-255147-0
1. Kissing   I. Title
GT2640.S2413   1992
394--dc20   92-10977

Design: Christian Diener
Editorial: Jenny Collins, Bill Messing, Laura Lindgren,
Jonathan Schwartz
Art Production: Joan K. Takenaka
Translations: Annalisa Ferguson, Magdalena Enea, Zack Rogow
Separations: Oestereicher + Wagner, Munich
Printing and Binding: Amilcare Pizzi S.p.A., Milan

For Sheytoun

Contents

Prologue

I was sitting in an airplane leafing through a magazine when a perfume advertisement caught my eye: a man pressing his lips against the neck of a woman whose eyes were half-closed. A mysterious smile played about her lips. Surreptitiously I glanced at the man seated next to me and saw that his gaze was drawn to the same advertisement. Our eyes met, and in his bright blue eyes a flash sparkled and danced as what seemed like an electric current passed between us, almost like telepathy: "Does it occur to you too that this ad is using a kiss to get our attention?" was all I could say. He couldn't suppress a smile, and thus began an intense discussion of the kiss, its different aspects, its meaning in general and for us in particular. We were captivated by the topic; unwaveringly our eyes held each other's gaze and our lips seemed eager to utter the word kiss again and again. The noise and everything else around us disappeared until the announcement of our imminent landing interrupted our conversation. In that instant, I felt an irresistible urge to put my head on my neighbor's shoulder and whisper in his ear, "One day I will give you one, I promise."

Here it is: my kiss for you.

Introduction

The mother kisses her baby
The athlete kisses his trophy
The handsome prince kisses Snow White
The serf kisses the hand of his lord
Lovers kiss each other
The patriot kisses the ground of his homeland
The superstitious kiss their talismans
The father kisses his son on the forehead
Doves bill and coo
The pious kiss their relics
The politician kisses his ally
The husband kisses his wife
The gambler kisses his cards
Don Juan seduces with a kiss
Judas kisses Jesus
The drunkard kisses his bottle
The little girl kisses her doll
With a kiss Pygmalion breathes life into a statue
Count Dracula kisses the neck of his victim
Romeo kisses Juliet till dawn
The saint kisses the leper's wounds
A mourner kisses his dear departed
The hobo kisses his dog
Clark Gable kisses Vivian Leigh in *Gone with the Wind*
The mother kisses away her child's pain
Saint Paul urges Christians to give the kiss of peace
In the Middle Ages a contract was sealed with a kiss
On February 14 you kiss your Valentine
Harlequin kisses Colombine before the eyes of the moonstruck Pierrot
Narcissus drowns trying to kiss his reflection

The Kiss Defined

The word "kiss" comes from the Greek word *kynéo*, which means to love or to kiss. According to *Pauly's Lexicon of Antiquity* it also means to greet or to embrace. The French word *baiser* comes from the Latin *basiare*, which is derived from the Sanskrit *bhadd*, to open the mouth. The Romans distinguished between various types of kisses according to their meaning and social function. To a friend one gave an *osculum*, to a relative a *basium*; a lover received a *suarium*. Modern dictionaries offer general definitions such as "to touch or press with the lips." In the 18th century Trévoux recorded a much more sensory definition of the kiss as "an attestation of friendship, love, respect, and humility that is given by pressing one's mouth to the cheek, face, or hand." *The Oxford English Dictionary* defines "kiss" as "To press or touch with the lips...in token of affection or greeting, or as an act of reverence..." All dictionary definitions, however, fall short in relating the many symbolic and sensory meanings of the act.

The Dictionary of Osculation suggests the possibilities. A play on an archaic English term for kissing, to buss, can be found under the title "Mind Your Own Bussiness."

Buss, a kiss.
Rebus, a kiss again.
Pluribus, to kiss irrespective of sex.
Syllabus, to kiss the hand instead of the lip.
Blunderbuss, to kiss the wrong person.
Erebus, to kiss in the dark.
Incubus, to have to kiss some one you don't like.
Harquebus, to kiss with a loud smack.

The German Brockhaus dictionary defines the kiss as follows: "To touch another person with the lips as an expression of love. A kiss on a woman's hand is an indication of respect or a social custom."

The linguists Jacob and Wilhelm Grimm covered numerous situations in their *German Dictionary*, beginning their definition with the kiss of friendship: "The kiss can express greeting, welcome, farewell, and the joy of reunion, and naturally, one cannot forget the kiss of love between a man and a woman."

The *Universal German Dictionary* defines the kiss more precisely: "To press one's lips against someone's mouth or cheek; if the kiss is not on the mouth or cheek, where one kisses another is always mentioned. Kissing can mean one or more kisses, whether given out of love, exuberance, as a sign of respect, or as a greeting. The phrase 'to give a kiss' means to kiss someone once on the mouth or cheek; it refers to a single completed action, sounds more informal, is generally less intense, and often implies a more noncommittal act than the phrase 'to kiss.'" The even more noncommittal, of course, can simply blow a kiss from the hand in someone else's general direction.

The multitude of meanings that the kiss has taken on in friendships, in rituals, and in the social relations of everyday life is explored at length in *The Kiss and Its History* by Christopher Nyrop. Nyrop elucidates over 30 kiss-related terms culled from a number of European dictionaries: the farewell kiss, kissing the bride, the brotherly kiss, the kiss of thanks, the double kiss, the kiss of honors, the return kiss, the fire kiss, the flame kiss, the kiss of women, the kiss of friendship, the kiss of peace, the ghost kiss, the kiss on the hand, the kiss of honey, the kiss of embrace, the kiss of Judas, the feudal kiss, the kiss of love, the kiss of girls, the poetic kiss, the morning kiss, the mother's kiss, the extra kiss, the kissing of slippers, the butterfly kiss, the first kiss, the kiss as blessing, the kiss of atonement, the kiss of innocence, the engagement kiss, the exchanged kiss, the inauguration kiss, the sugar kiss, and on and on. To that list might be added any number of modern alternatives: to kiss goodnight, kiss and make up, kiss the ground, kiss off, kiss ass, the kiss of death, kissing cousins…kiss goodbye.

The Kiss in French and Its Double Meaning

Since the 17th century the French word *baiser* has been used to mean two things: either to give a kiss or to have sex with someone. The word was once considered taboo, which is precisely why the great dramatists of the period such as Corneille, Racine, and Molière used it to get a laugh out of their audiences. The double meaning of the word lent itself especially well to ribald and risqué puns. Molière played with this *double entendre* in *Don Juan*: superficially the meaning seems rather prim and proper, yet at the same time the word expresses exactly what one has in mind but dare not say.

The Kiss from Antiquity to the Present

From cradle to grave, throughout our entire lives the kiss accompanies all our most intense emotional experiences. And yet behind this activity, which has been practiced virtually worldwide since time immemorial, there often lies a paradox.

From the maternal kiss that gives security, warmth, and life to the newborn to the "kiss of death" the Mafioso presses against the lips of one he has sentenced to die; from Romeo's passionate kiss uniting him with Juliet to the insincere peck on the cheek between sophisticated ex-lovers; from the kiss of humility the Pope annually bestows on the feet of a poor pilgrim to the kiss by which Judas betrayed Jesus; from the sensual kiss

of the experienced courtesan to the fleeting kiss blown from the fingertips—the fundamental expression of love, tenderness, and respect contained in this single gesture can be transformed in innumerable symbolic and meaningful ways.

There is a fundamental difference between the intimate, loving, or erotic kiss, which signals closeness, and that which is intended to express respect, alliance, or admiration in public. Early chronicles describe only the ritual kiss of submission and prayer. The earliest examples of this are found in Mesopotamian depictions of the worship of the god Larsa: engraved on a cylindrical vessel are people kissing the god's hand. In Mesopotamian culture the mouth was considered holy and there were laws punishing the misuse of a kiss. Thus it was that a beautiful Babylonian woman who dared to kiss her husband's hunting companion in public had both her ears cut off, while her passionate accomplice paid for his impertinence with the loss of his upper lip.

The Egyptians, decidedly more civilized, scented their mouths with herbs and honey candies to make their kisses taste better.

The ancient Persians exchanged different types of kisses according to their social standing. According to Herodotus, "This is a way to find out whether the people who meet one another are of the same social status: instead of greeting each other with words, they kiss each other on the mouth. If one of them is of a slightly lower social status, they kiss each other on the cheeks. However, if one of them is of far lower birth, he must throw himself down before the other and kiss the dust from his feet."

Even the Greeks, who adopted certain Persian customs after they were conquered by Alexander the Great, practiced the ritual kiss. They primarily employed the kiss blown from the hand as a sign of worship of a deity or of respect for a person.

The Roman emperors, who in so many areas imitated the Greeks, ordered their subjects to kiss the imperial statues as though they were holy. Cicero reported that this order was obeyed to such excess that in some cases the lips and chins of the statues were worn down. This practice of continual kissing became so unbearable that the emperor Tiberius banned the public kiss. Fortunately this did not extend to the other two forms of kiss, *basium*, the kiss among family members, and *suavium*, the kiss between lovers.

The satirist Martial made the following observation:

Impossible! From this forever gaping
And kissing crowd there can be no escaping,
No matter how your fate you may be shaping.
No epidemic, no contagion shunning,
And not afraid of the most mortal punning,
They after you with kisses will be running.
And their eternal kisses you'll be getting
E'en when your nose in summer heat is sweating,
Or when it with a cold its drops are letting.
No hat or hood will be your forehead shielding.
You are not safe, though you a sword be wielding,
For never, never, never they be yielding.
They know and use a thousand new devices,
And at each turn you surely meet a crisis.
A kissing brother knows no place or station
Where you may rest, and knowing no cessation
He will pursue you through the whole creation.

When Christianity replaced ancient traditions, the kiss took on a new dimension through the words of Saint Paul, *"Salutate invicem osculo sancto,"* a call to believers urging them to greet each other with the holy kiss. The *Dictionary of Christian Antiquity and Liturgy* emphasizes the importance of this message: "For Saint Paul, the kiss seems to have become a special symbol of brotherhood among Christians, not just a show of affection but an indication of shared feelings and beliefs. Thus this kiss was holy."

The sacred nature of the kiss was most pronounced in the courtly kiss widespread among knights of the Middle Ages. Every knight was obliged to select the lady of his heart, to whom he would express a purely Platonic love that could never cross the boundary of the kiss.

During the Renaissance, courtly love became more sophisticated and took many forms. People still kissed each other on the mouth as a greeting and on other occasions, but the Plague brought an end to this custom as doctors began to recognize the risk of contagion through breath and saliva. Following the puritanical trend of the times, during the 17th century the kiss remained a part of social custom, but the lips touched only the hand or the cheek. This development persists to the present day, in which the kiss on the mouth is restricted to intimate relationships between two people. Only in Russia is it still customary for one person to greet another formally by pressing his lips against those of the other.

The Kiss as Breath of Life

Not only lips and tongues are united and surrender to each other in a kiss. An invisible element is exchanged by two kissing people as well: breath.

In speaking of breath, the soul comes to mind, and thus God. The Holy Scripture tells us that God infused life into the first human being with his breath. Breath is the fundamental element of life that allows creation to repeat again and again. The invitation "Let him kiss me with the kisses of his mouth" expressed in the Song of Songs suggests an inseparable consent between two spirits.

We think of Pygmalion, who breathed life into a statue with his kiss but presumably soon came to regret it—certainly much sooner than did the god Pan who persistently pursued the nymph Syrinx. When she transformed into a reed to escape him, he simply cut the reed and whittled it into a flute so that he could bring her to his lips whenever he liked and play any song that popped into his head.

Every kiss from him creates desire
His perfumed breath fans the fire of love
Awakens the embers from their slumber:
How I would love to be such a kiss.

Every religion defines the role and spiritual meaning of the kiss. In the Bible the kiss has countless functions. In the Old Testament it is represented as a means of emotional exchange between the members of a family. The *Jewish Encyclopedia* says: "Isaac desires to kiss Esau; Esau falls upon Jacob's neck and kisses him; Joseph kisses his brethren and the face of his dead father...Elisha desires to kiss his father and mother before following Elijah."

The Kiss of Peace

An early form of the spiritual kiss is the kiss of peace, which is first mentioned by St. Justin Martyr (second century A.D.).

In early Christian times, the kiss stood for a deep bond between believers: it conveyed a feeling of unity and belonging in heart and spirit. According to Abbot Barraud, "the ceremony of the kiss of peace obviously had no drawbacks in an age when belief was strong and morals pure." In the Middle Ages men and women routinely kissed each other on the mouth. One can imagine that religious ceremony was not necessarily the primary motivation. As a social act the kiss was thus frequently abused, and it was soon considered immoral. A Catholic encyclopedia gives this explanation: "We have definite evidence that a kiss was on some occasions bestowed outside the actual liturgy." This is why Pope Innocent III forbade mouth-to-mouth kissing and decreed that henceforth only persons of the same sex might exchange the kiss of peace.

To this day the kiss of peace has been preserved in most liturgical rituals, as in baptism, or in the ordination of a priest by a bishop.

Other forms of kisses have been completely lost, such as the kiss given to the dead to become the repository of the soul. Because even in this custom there arose cases of misuse, the Magistrate of Auxerre forbade the practice in A.D. 578.

The Kiss of Exorcism

The spirit of the kiss has led to superstitious beliefs in the popular traditions of all cultures. When a child falls down, immediately we kiss the hurt spot and make it better. This custom comes from a formerly common practice of sucking the poison from a wound. To this day the phrase "Suck out the bad!" is still used by some tribes in Africa, Australia, India, America, and among the Eskimos.

Gamblers used to kiss their cards before the beginning of a game to bring them luck.

To cure a toothache, kiss a donkey on the cheek.

To protect yourself from lightning, cross yourself and kiss the ground three times.

In Greenland, mothers kiss their children in the

THE KISS
OF
LOVE

How shall we define a kiss?
The sacrament of a vow, the lightly stamped seal of a promise,
the endorsement of a promissory note on the bank of love,
the very O of love in the expectant lips…

Edmond Rostand

*Ten kisses are
more easily forgotten
than one kiss.*

Jean Paul

*The lips of a woman
are the most beautiful
gate to her soul.*

Chinese proverb

There are things,
which can only be said while kissing,
because the deepest and
purest things might not come from the heart
if not summoned by a kiss.

Maurice Maeterlinck

Print thy lips Into the ayre
So by this Meanes I may kisse thy kisse
When as some kinde winde
Shall hither waft it and In liew
My lips shall send 1000 back to you.

Robert Herrick

*I kissed you in the car. My fingers felt
cruel as they caressed your hair. I didn't
tremble, I didn't get in over my head. Of that
I'm sure. There was your mouth, voraciously
open to my kiss. "Drunk," I was thinking,
"drunk and knowledgeable, and so good…"
Already doubt, mistrust, and pleasure were
mixed. You were unwinding as if asleep.
Your body was long, softened, chaste,
I didn't dare touch you. Only this: your
mouth, that adolescent kiss just past, the
vague and hot taste of the wine you'd sipped,
my head spinning when I closed my eyes.
At the end of our breath we separated our
half-opened lips. "Diane kisses," I thought.
Just the way soldiers would point out to each
other a bistro sign—"Josette's is closing up"—
or the way people say admiringly, "Brigitte
rides," or "Helene plays bridge." This kiss
became a social skill, an unexpected sporting
event. So you knew the tango, cars, veils and
kisses. And I was ashamed. I remembered
the esteem in which I held you. Under the
pretext of loving you, how had I treated
you? How many women had I kissed in that
car? How many hands had I caressed,
how many fingers counted as a game,
gestures sliding in the dark—and under
mine, lips saying no?*

François Nourissier

What of the soul was left, I wonder,
when the kissing had to stop?

Robert Browning

They sat down on the bench.
They were not able to find the words.
How could it be that
their lips found one another?
How could it be that a bird was singing,
that the snow was melting,
that a rose was opening?

Victor Hugo

And just as some people
spend 100 francs a day on a hotel room
in Balbec to breathe the sea air,
I found it natural to spend even more than that on her,
since her breath was on my cheek,
in my half-open mouth which I pressed on hers,
where her life glided along my tongue.

Marcel Proust

*And the best
and the worst of this is,
That neither is most to blame,
If you have forgotten my kisses
And I have forgotten
your name.*

Algernon Charles Swinburne

Each kiss calls forth another.
Ah! in the first days of love, kisses
come so naturally! They multiply so quickly,
one after the other; and it would be as
difficult to count the kisses they gave each
other in the course of an hour as
it would be to number the flowers in
a field in May.

Marcel Proust

THE MOTHER'S KISS

Worlds emerged from the echo of a kiss.
Amado Nervo

The Kiss of Life

The first kiss we know is our mother's. It is a sort of welcoming kiss that most of us receive, and this moment is certainly one of the most intense and magical of our lives. It lasts perhaps only a second, but it remains an irreplaceable treasure for the rest our lives: the experience of tenderness. This very first kiss also marks our first emotional and physical contact. We feel our mother's warmth and protection. We hear her heartbeat, which conveys the feeling of security. The scent of the bodies of our mother and father guides us wordlessly, sightlessly. Above all, we feel loved.

Frequently this first kiss is connected to the natural need for nourishment: nourishment not just in the form of sustenance but tenderness as well. One theory about the origin of the kiss maintains that it arose from the necessity of feeding. In an article entitled "The Origin of the Kiss," the 19th-century Italian anthropologist Cesare Lombroso stated: "I think the kiss originates in a maternal action, the act of feeding, in the way that birds feed their young. We know that this is the normal way in which the inhabitants of Tierra del Fuego give their infants a drink, since drinking vessels are unknown there. An adult drinks directly from a brook with a reed. A child would die of thirst if the mother did not give him water to drink by transferring it directly from her mouth to his.

"In the past, before the advent of special baby-food manufacturing techniques, a mother fed her child by first chewing a mouthful of food, and then pushing it in her child's mouth. This naturally led to an intense interplay of lips and tongues. Even today this practice is common among primitive peoples. Of course, the idea that this tender gesture emerged from the ways in which birds and human beings ingested their food is neither particularly romantic nor erotic. To this day the mouth-to-mouth feeding of children is still practiced by the Indians of the Amazon. The first kiss probably arose from this behavior, which is actually more maternal than erotic."

Kiss and Smell

Our first encounter with the world is oral: crying followed by nursing. Crying announces hunger and thirst, and nursing satisfies these natural needs. For mother and child alike, feeding does far more than supply nourishment; it is a form of tenderness and pleasure. Freudian analysis goes a step further in the erotic domain: the joy of nursing is associated with the complete focus of attention, which leads either to falling asleep or even to a neural response in the nature of orgasm.

The kiss is closely intertwined with the sense of smell. Even today among certain peoples the customary manner of greeting is to sniff one another's cheeks. The Burmese say "smell me" instead of "kiss me." The two expressions "to kiss" and "to smell" are often confused, since when we kiss someone we first register the smell of the skin. Babies have a very pronounced olfactory sense and can recognize their mothers by smell alone. Nursing and smelling are united in an inseparable whole. Freud called this an eroticization of the mouth.

The maternal kiss is vital to the child. This gesture of affection, which we so often take for granted, conveys a sense of security that is essential to the child. Children discover that the reward for good behavior is a kiss from a parent. And what happens when they are naughty? They are forgiven with a kiss as well. Through this kiss of reconciliation a thousand things are silently expressed. One must learn to interpret kisses, because within them lie many hidden messages. The kiss, in any event, is an effective educational tool, for it is through tenderness that children most easily come to understand their mistakes. By the same token, children are often able to express their feelings with a kiss when words fail them. The maternal kiss imparts security and shows them that they are not alone. This is why the goodnight kiss is so important to children.

In *Remembrance of Things Past*, Marcel Proust described his childhood memories thus: "My sole consolation when I went upstairs for the night was that Mamma would come in and kiss me after I was in bed....So much did I love that goodnight that I reached the stage of hoping that it would come as late as possible, so as to prolong the period during which Mamma had not yet appeared."

Parents, too, need this kiss, for it gives them strength in knowing they are loved. The innocent, sincere, simple kiss of one's child is a powerful testimony of love. And the kiss children deny when they sulk and feign indifference hurts just as much as the opposite pleases.

Children are more sensitive to a lack of tenderness than adults. Depending on their individual sensitivities and other circumstances, this deficiency can lead to severe disorders.The following excerpt from Jules Renard's diary describes a communication gap between father and son regarding the kiss:

He never returns my kiss. It would call for a great internal upheaval in him, which I do not foresee occurring now or in the future. When the moment comes to say goodbye, he is as silent as am I for a long time before. Then suddenly he says, "Well, then," and reaches his hand out to me. I approach him. He always recoils a little, for he understands immediately. Surely he is saying to himself, "Well, now he wants to kiss me." But when I pull him toward me, he does not protest. What a strange kiss, so strong and yet so cold, useless and yet so necessary. The kiss of uninvolved lips on a cheek that has no taste, neither of skin nor of wood. He feels nothing on his cheek and I feel nothing on my lips. It makes me shudder. Our fathers do not urge us to hug them. They are linked to us through invisible bonds and subterranean roots.

Renard's observations would not seem at all surprising to someone Chinese. In China, a father never kisses his son and does not, in turn, expect to be kissed by his son either.

Kierkegaard described a farewell kiss that imparts strength: "She looked so young and fresh, as if nature like a tender and opulent mother had that very instant released her from her hand. It seemed to me as if I had been witness to this farewell scene; I marked how the loving mother once again embraced her and bade her farewell; I heard her say: 'Go out into the world now, my child; I have done all for you. Now take this kiss as a seal upon your lips; 'tis a seal the sanctuary preserves; no one can break it against your will, but when the right man comes, you shall understand him.' And she presses a kiss on her lips—a kiss which, not like a human kiss, takes aught, but a divine kiss that gives all. The chaste purity, which is Cordelia's halo and protection, is, as it were, the reflection of a mother's kiss."

I dreamt
I covered my mother
with kisses and that
she was naked.

Stendhal

My kiss will give peace now
And quiet to your heart—
Sleep on in peace now,
O you unquiet heart!

James Joyce

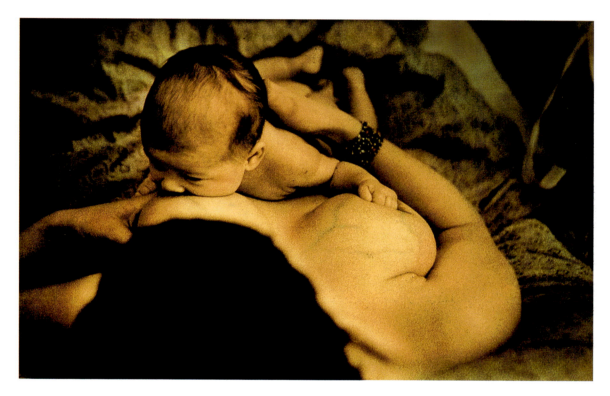

For a glance, the world;
for a smile, the heavens,
for a kiss...I do not know
what I would give you for a kiss!
Gustavo Adolfo Bécquer

Kiss our beloved child
And you will feel warmth and peace.
I shower you with all my love,
Light of my life...

Czarina Alexandra to Czar Nicholas II,
Tsarkoye Selo, December 4, 1916

THE KISS
IN
NATURE

*It is remarkable that
human beings, turtle doves, and doves are
the only beings which kiss.*

Voltaire

Breathless, we flung us on the windy hill,
Laughed in the sun, and kissed the lovely grass.

Rupert Brooke

*Tenderness is
a blossom to be plucked
from the lips.*

M.S.

The moth's kiss first!
Kiss me as if you made believe
You were not sure, this eve,
How my face, your flower, had pursed
Its petals up; so here and there
You brush it, till I grow aware
Who wants me, and wide ope I burst.

Robert Browning

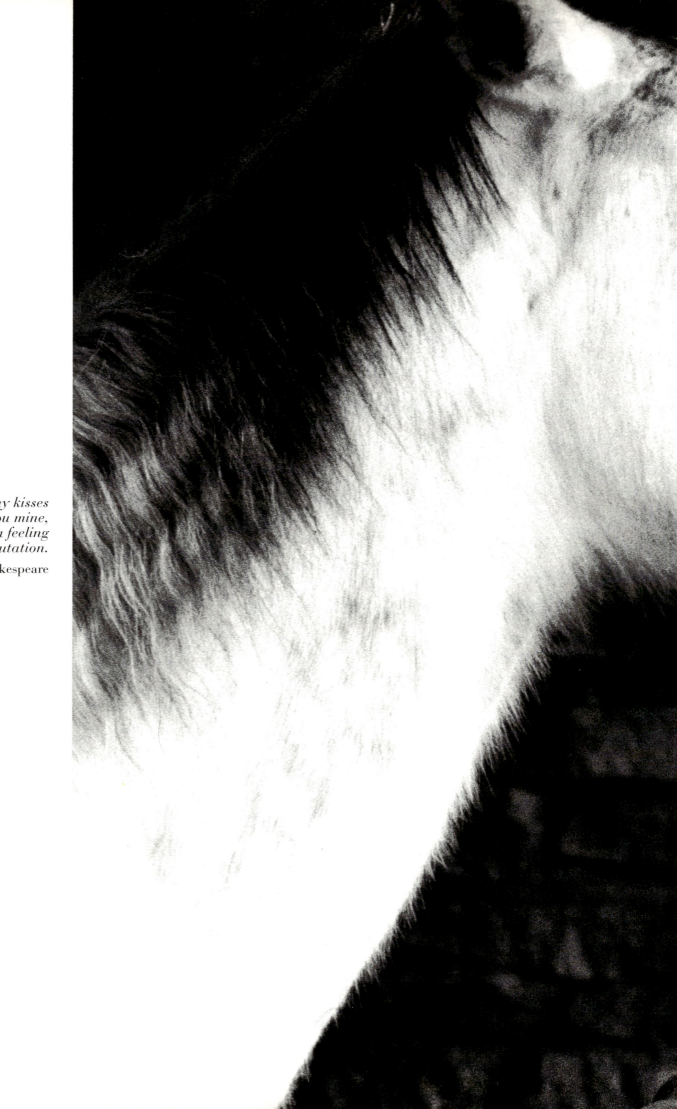

*I understand thy kisses
and thou mine,
And that's a feeling
disputation.*

William Shakespeare

It is by the nose
that one breathes, it is by
the nose that we sense
the breath of the one
we love; it seems to us that
we mingle our soul
with hers.

Javanese painter

Kiss me, or I will kiss you!
Johann Wolfgang von Goethe

THE PLAYFUL KISS

His kisses—feel like paradise
as when two flames embrace one another,
as when harp tones play intertwined unto the
heavens full of harmony.

Friedrich von Schiller

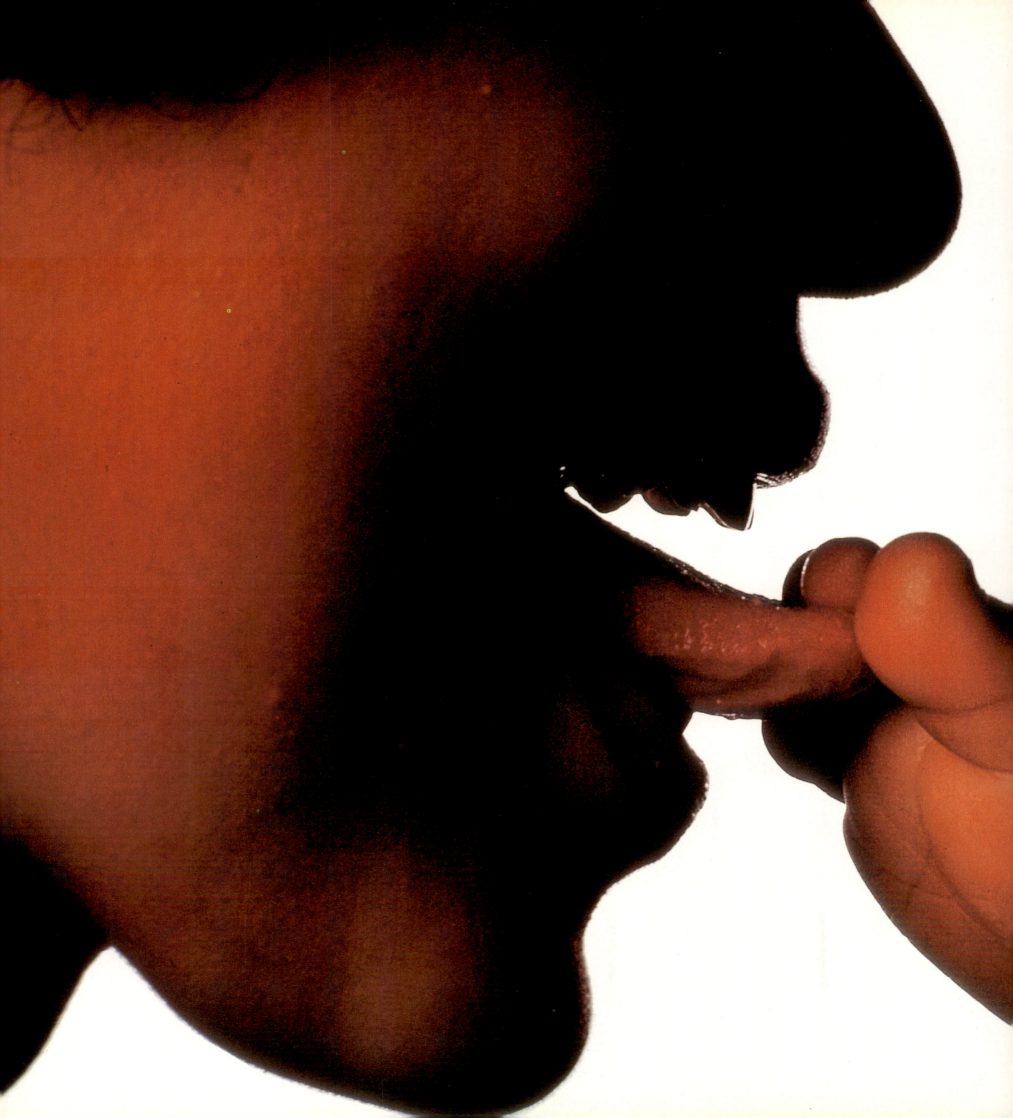

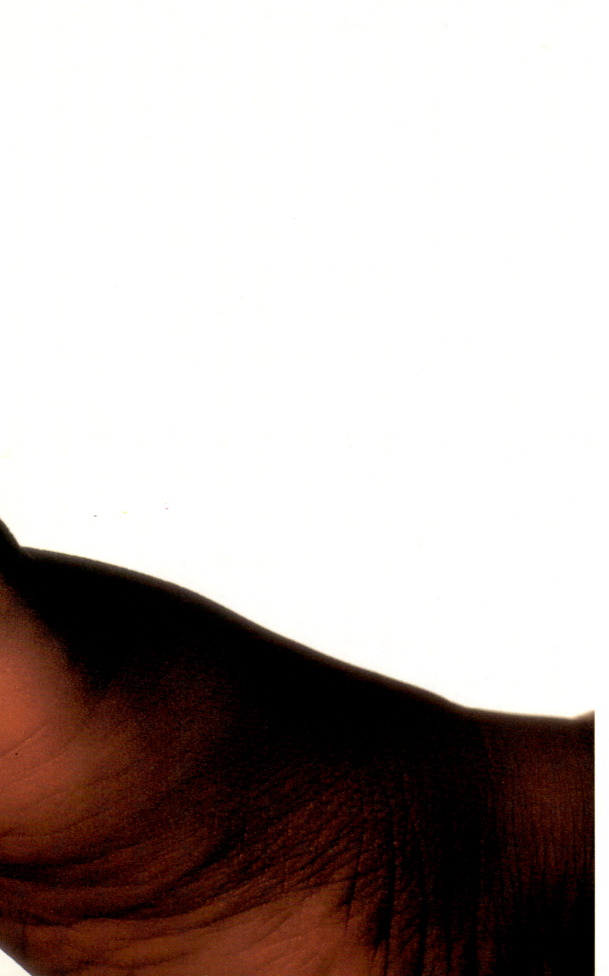

Comedy in Three Caresses

She hadn't much left on, and the big trees
With no discretion, swished
Their leaves over the window-pane
Teasingly, so near, so near.

Half naked in my big chair,
She put her hands together
And her little toes tickled the floor,
Quivering comfortably, and so small.

I watched a little sprouting flush,
The color of wax, flutter
Like a smile over her neat breasts:
Fly on a rose bush.

I kissed her traced ankles
And she smiled a longish smile, bad sign
That shattered out into clear trills,
Crystalline.

Her little feet scampered under her shift:
"Will you stop now!!"
After the first permitted boldness,
The smile pretending coldness?

Her poor eyelids fluttered under my lips
As I kissed her eyes
And she threw back her weakling head:
"That's better now," she said.

"But I have something still to…"
I chucked the rest between her breasts
In a caress that brought a kindly smile,
Benevolence, all of it.

She hadn't much left on, and the big trees
Swished their leaves over the window-pane
At ease, teasingly, and so near.

                                Arthur Rimbaud

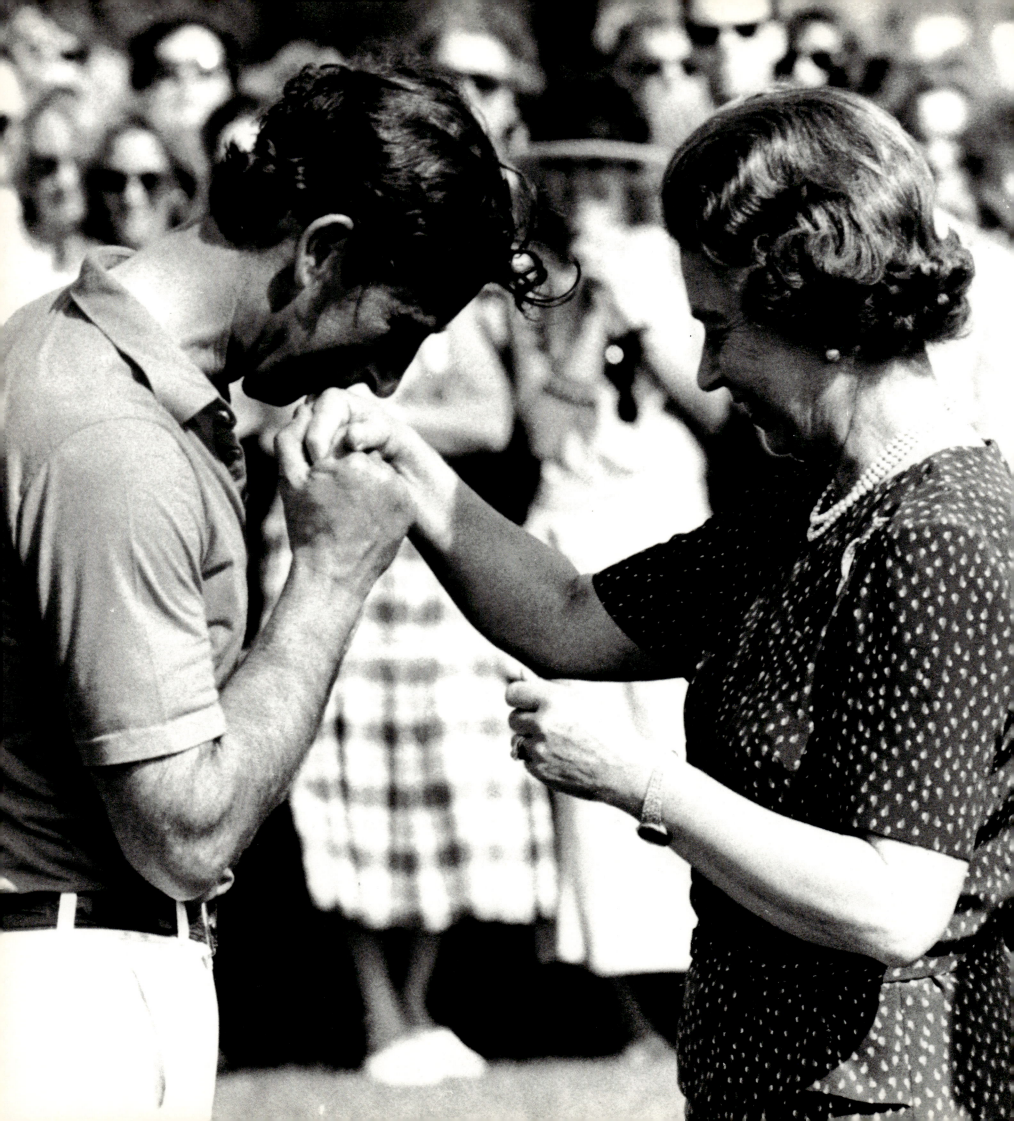

THE KISS AS SOCIAL RITUAL

What is a kiss?
Why this, as some approve:
The sure, sweet cement,
glue and lime of love.

Robert Herrick

Drink to me
only with thine eyes,
And I will pledge
with mine;
Or leave a kiss but
in the cup
And I'll not look
for wine.

Ben Jonson

*Fame is not a lover
you can ever neglect,
and you must also prove worthy of
the first marks of her favors
if you hope always
to receive more of the same.*

Louis XIV

He who binds himself to joy
Does the winged life destroy;
But he who kisses joy as it flies
Lives in eternity's sunrise.

William Blake

*One can hardly
begin discussing kissing
before words emerge
that are not found
in the dictionary of
the academy.*

Prosper Mérimée

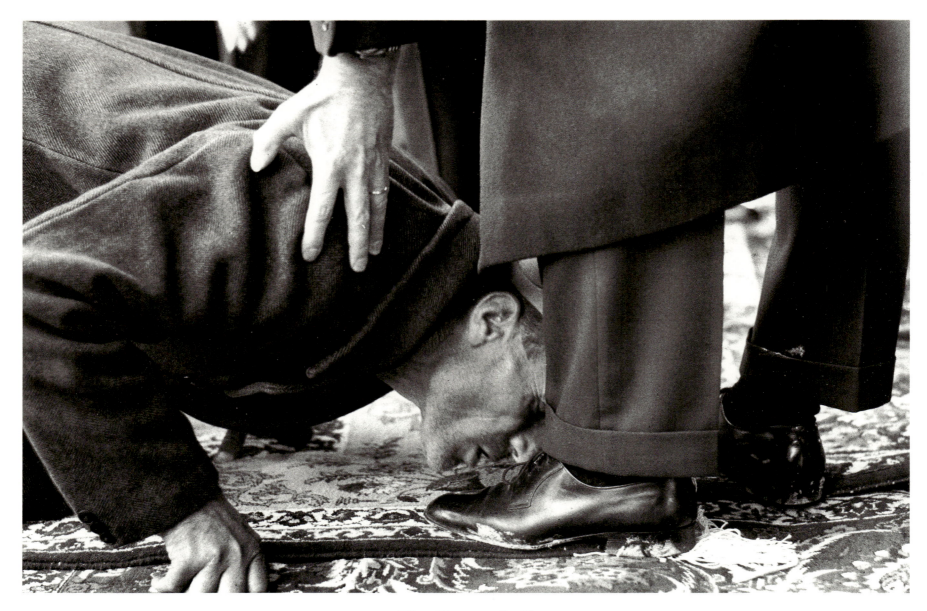

"*He will return, I will*
give him back to you, and I want
you to be grateful to me
lifelong for this, and to love him
out of love for me. I will do
even more, I will make him a Field
Marshall in my army."
The brother, not knowing how to
express his joy and gratitude,
threw himself at the king's feet and
hugged his knees. The king
raised him up and said, "This is not
how brothers should kiss,"
and embraced him.

Madame de Sévigné to Bussy-Rabutin

Kisses belong to the shadows,
but they shine in the night like stars.
Rémy de Gourmont

I close your ear with kisses
And seal your nostrils, and round your neck you'll wear—
Nay, let me work—a delicate chain of kisses.
Like beads they go around, and not one misses
To touch its fellow on either side.

D. H. Lawrence

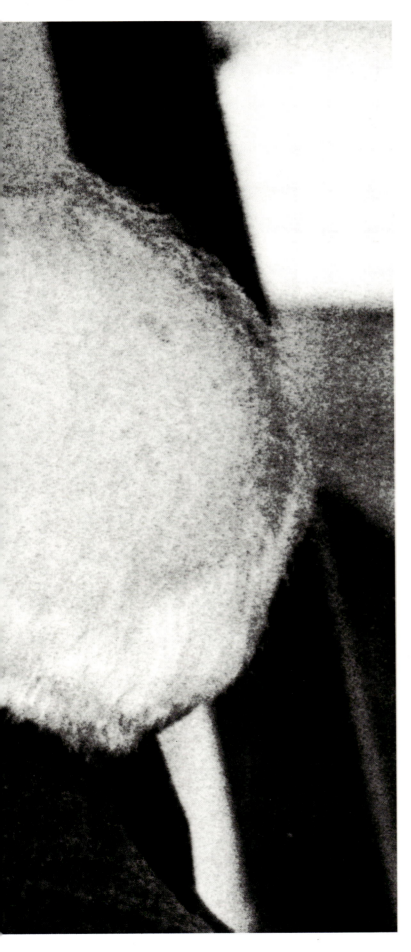

If only I knew
what fizzles in my soul,
Words and kisses
are so wonderfully mixed.

Heinrich Heine

Yet each man kills the thing he loves,
By each let this be heard,
Some do it with a bitter look,
Some with a flattering word.
The coward does it with a kiss,
The brave man with a sword!

Oscar Wilde

THE KISS IN MOVIES

*ROMEO: Then move not while
my prayers' effect I take. (He kisses her) Thus
from my lips, by thine, my sin is purg'd.
JULIET: Then have my lips the sin that they have took.
ROMEO: Sin from my lips? O trespass sweetly urg'd!
Give me my sin again. (Kisses her again)
JULIET: You kiss by th' book.*

William Shakespeare

"Kiss me, Phil, please. Please…"
He kissed her, blending with his
own pleasure the inept clumsiness
of extreme youth that looks no
further than the gratification of
its own desires, and the all too
precise memory of a kiss that
other lips had taken from his,
though not simply for the asking.
But pressed to his lips he felt the
form and shape of Vinca's mouth,
still tasting of the fruit she had
just bitten into, felt the eagerness
of her lips to open and discover
their secret that they might
squander its sweetness on his—
and he swayed in the darkness.
"I really believe we are lost,"
he thought. "Oh, let it happen
quickly, since it must, and since
she now could never wish
it to be otherwise. Oh God, how
wonderful and inevitable her
mouth is, and so understanding,
right from the start! Oh, let it
happen quickly, quickly…"

Colette

When you offer me closed kisses with tight lips
and from your mouth no breath comes, an indefinable
sadness steals into my mind and our very kisses grow cold
in our silent mouths. But when snatched kisses resound on
biting lips and mingled breaths unite in each other's
mouths, color and soul and sense desert me, and I myself
lie fainting on your breasts.

Now place your tongue between my lips and
keep it ever warm within my mouth, lest passageways
be made for the soul, lest the cold tongue stiffen
and myself expire upon your breast.

Giovanni Pontano

*How disgusting it always is
to kiss in front of a third person!*

Plutarch

And the magic of
his words, his hands and,
Oh! his kiss!

Gone is my peace,
my heart is heavy and I will
never find it again.

My heart longs for him,
and if I were able to touch
and hold him

And kiss him
as I will, then would I die of
his kisses!

Johann Wolfgang von Goethe

A long, long kiss, a kiss of youth and love
And beauty, all concentrating like rays
Into one focus, kindled from above;
Such kisses as belong to early days,
Where heart, and soul, and sense, in concert move,
And the blood's lava, and the pulse a blaze,
Each kiss a heart-quake—for a kiss's strength
I think, it must be reckon'd by its length.

Lord Byron

A kiss on your heart,
and then a little lower,
much, much lower.

Napoleon Bonaparte to Josephine

Dreamed-Up for Winter

This winter in a rosy railroad car
With blue upholstery
We shall be snug. Nestsful of kisses are
Waiting for us in every padded cranny.

You with your eyes shut tight so you won't see
Evening shadows—
Demons, black wolves and cross monstrosities
Glare through the windows.

Then on your cheek a scratch or something lighter
A tiny kiss which runs like a panicked spider
Downward somewhere out of touch...

And you will tell me "Look for it!" with a gesture.
And we will take our time finding this creature
—Who moves about so much...

Arthur Rimbaud

She drew him to
her with her eyes.
He put his face
against hers,
placed his lips
against hers,
which were like a
freshly cut fig.
Kamala kissed
him deeply, and to
Siddhartha's great
astonishment he
felt how much she
taught him, how
clever she was,
how she mastered
him, repulsed him,
lured him, and
how after this long
kiss, a long series
of other kisses, all
different, awaited
him. He stood still
breathing deeply.
At that moment
he was like a child
astonished at
the fullness of
knowledge and
learning which
unfolded itself
before his eyes.

Hermann Hesse

O kiss me yet again, O kiss me over
And over! Kiss me this time tenderly;
And this time let your passion enter me
And burn me through! I shall return, my lover,

Four more for every one you give me—yes,
Ten more if you desire it, still more tender.
Dreamy and drugged with kisses we shall wander
Through all our utter, intermingled bliss!

And so in each of us two lives have grown
Concealed in one: our lover's, and our own.
A paradox has gathered in my brain:

For while my life is disciplined and lonely,
My heart is ill, and can recover only
When it escapes, and breaks in two again.

Louise Labé

The splashing of waves
on a pebbled beach is like the
sound of long kisses.

Johannes Jørgensen

For the lips that kissed me, these tender, cool, impersonal lips are the same as yesterday and their ineffectiveness annoys me...But suddenly they change and I no longer recognize the kiss: it becomes lively, demanding, then tender, and then again feverish, withdraws a little and again becomes more urgent and rhythmic and suddenly it pauses, as if waiting for an answer that does not come...

Colette

How delicious is the winning
Of a kiss at Love's beginning,
When two mutual hearts are sighing
For the knot there's no untying!

Thomas Campbell

THE KISS IN ART

Thus the lover spoke: "Come hither,
Come and suck from lips a-blooming
Youthful folly, sin and sweetness!
Come, and from the chaliced lily
of my bosom drink the vital
strength that life anew is giving."

Hafiz

In the vibrant interplay of colors
in the mosaic of forms
two bodies melt together
two arms entwine,
two heads come close together
two hands touch
and two faces merge
into one.

M.S.

In delay there lies no plenty;
Then come kiss me, sweet and twenty,
Youth's a stuff will not endure.

William Shakespeare

If I die in your arms my lady,
I am happy;
therefore I wish to have
no greater honor in the world
than to see myself,
while kissing you, give up my
soul in your breast.

Pierre de Ronsard

A piece of jewelry that
carries inside
the perfect and pure way
to togetherness
brought to life by
a heartbeat.

M.S.

You pressed your lips upon my lips,
Your heart upon my beating heart;
But all my trust and pride in you
Lie crushed and shattered now, alas.

Bahadur Shah Zafar

What has the dark infinite crafted best
For the dwellers of the earth?
What is our father's masterpiece?
What is the lightning of the heavens?
Resting my head, under the clouds
Her unbreakable wings
Between which she is nude
Psyche said to me: "It's the kiss."

Victor Hugo

The Magical Kiss

A rainy day
a magical day
overwhelming tenderness
and a yearning look.

Our bodies are drawn to each other
like two magnets
and we dream of life like two lovers.
He touches my lips so tenderly
and lures me
into the secret garden of delights.
His warmth and his scent
intoxicate me
and I lose all senses.
I close my eyes to feel his embrace
and the wild beating of my heart.

M.S.

Silence now. We've come
to a downward sloping path. Anabel
walks pressed against me like a mischievous
sister, a daughter of summer. She raises
her eyes in that insistent way of hers. We take a
fork toward a green nook surrounded by
cypresses. I grasp her arm, she frees
herself. I kiss her. Our hands cross with twin
destinations. Lying in the grass I see
her black enticing eyes and the naked skin of
her legs under the hiked skirt. "I'll tell
you what you need…" Nocturnal gestures
under bright sunlight. An embrace
that could perhaps bring on tears, and in
the light her lips are purple, her hand,
which digs at the grass also digs
into me, her mouth has the taste of
fresh grass and of the past, a childhood
smell which has returned with
the scent of the cypresses.

Marc Lambron

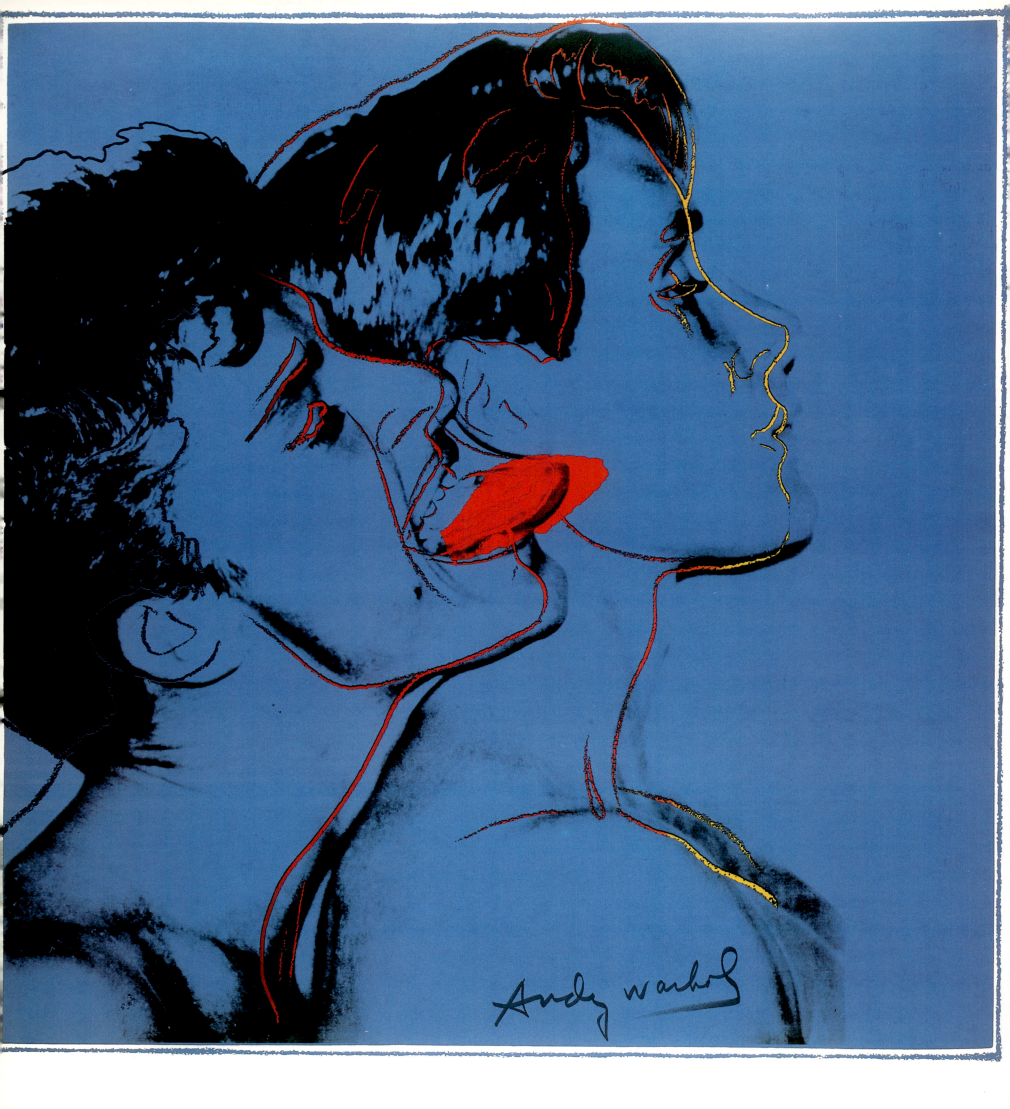

Mouths longing to kiss
Tongues thirsting to lick
Devour me in your desire
like prey
that trembles with lust.

M.S.

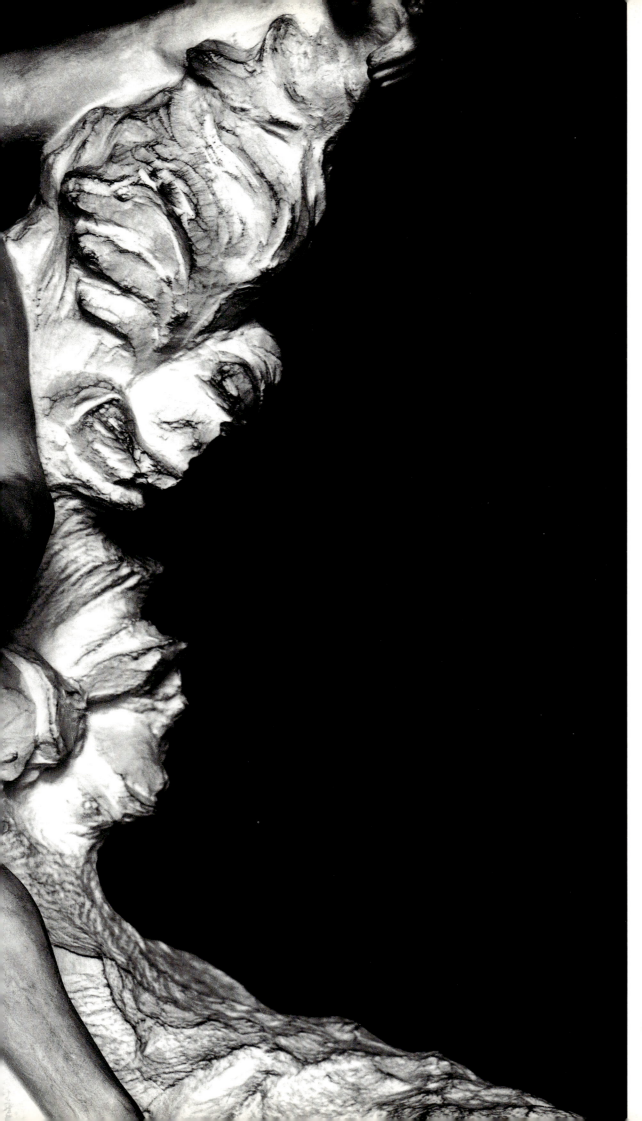

Take, O take those lips away,
That so sweetly were forsworn,
And those eyes: the break of day,
Lights that do mislead the morn:
But my kisses bring again, bring again,
Seals of love, but seal'd in vain, seal'd in vain.

William Shakespeare

THE EROTIC KISS

The kiss is the son of two caressing lips,
Daughter of two rosebuds.

Pierre de Ronsard

The Kiss and Desire

In earlier times, even through the first half of this century, yearning for a kiss from one's beloved meant kissing on the cheek, the neck, or the shoulder. Erotic feelings were expressed mostly in the yearning itself. In the forties, a hit song could still carry the refrain: "I kiss your hand, Madame"; the eroticism lay in the expression, in the timbre, and in the movements of the singer.

Today the kiss is the language of eroticism. It is a symbolic gesture of union in which lovers immerse themselves, holding a passionate dialogue that arises from or leads to ecstasy. The kiss of love is exchanged at the moment when physical passion reaches its climax. It is an all-consuming way to express our love and desire. All-consuming and yet never-ending, as Else Lasker-Schüler declared in verses: "Listen! We must kiss each other intensely. A yearning of which we must all die knocks on the door of the world."

The kiss of love is also a bodily act of union, a carnal act, for the simple reason that the human mouth is a highly sensuous and sensitive organ. Although the kiss often serves as foreplay to an act of love, there are also love games without kisses. And a kiss can be erotic even if it has nothing to do with actually making love.

The kiss punctuates love's sentences, bringing expression to the deepest of feelings. In *Les Deux Baisers*, Achille Tatius described how erotic kisses enhance sexual desire:

It is desire to which you unconditionally surrender; the kiss impresses itself on the lips like a seal in wax. Desire knows how to enhance the sweetness of kisses. It is not enough for the lips to unite lovingly; the teeth, too, long to embrace. Desire devours the mouth of her lover; she bites while kissing. Her breasts, through which one hears her heartbeat in one's hand, are a new source of desire. In the highest moment of love she quivers as if stung by desire; her mouth opens to a stream of kisses; she loses all control. These are the moments when tongues seek each other; they, too, want to unite and embrace. Pleasure is heightened if lips are parted for long, deep kisses. Toward the end, the woman grows breathless with a passion that overwhelms her. Her heavy breathing mixes with the breath of love on her lips, upon which she receives the kiss that wants to penetrate ever deeper until it becomes one with her and touches her deep in her heart.

The taste of the kiss is critical to its sensual effect. In *A Thousand and One Nights* the sultan,

May your kiss have the fire of the sun.   Kurdistan proverb

embracing the princess of the sea, wants to taste the saliva of her exquisite mouth. Included in these stories are many descriptions of kisses:

His juice is more desirable than the juice of grapes, it quenches the most burning thirst, such is his mouth.

Ah! When I taste his lips! Oh! This juice, which flows from ripe grapes even before they are pressed. Look! Honey which flows from under pearls!

Not surprisingly, even in Nefertiti's time there were sweet, aromatic pastilles to make the breath fragrant and kisses more appealing.

In Solomon's Song of Songs 4:11, the taste of the kiss is described:

Thy lips, O my spouse, drop as the honeycomb; honey and milk are under thy tongue; and the smell of thy garments is like the smell of Lebanon.

In Persian poetry, the desirability of the lips and their taste is described as even more delectable than kisses. In the great love story *Leili and Majnoun* by Nézami, told in verse, a lover dreams of possessing the taste of Leili's kisses:

Her ruby mouth demands kisses; promising to be soft and sugar-sweet, as sweet as a honeycomb...

Such comparisons between a kiss and the choicest of all imaginable aromas, such as those of wine, sugar and honey, appear often in literature as a means of evocatively depicting the kisses of lovers stolen or longed for. The reader tastes their sweetness on the lips, feels the familiar intoxication of the wine.

The Erotic Kiss in the Orient

The origin of the erotic kiss lies in the distant past, as the art of eroticism existed even in ancient Eastern cultures. The kiss was exchanged primarily in sexually loaded situations. In the Arab world, the kiss is synonymous with sexual desire. The ethics of Islam detail the rules concerning the time, place, and manner in which a kiss may be given. It is an impure act to exchange a kiss outside matrimony. During Ramadan, the month of fasting, even married couples are obliged to forgo kissing.

Above all, the kiss remains an act of foreplay, a pledge to the passion of eroticism and love. It can also be a tool of revenge. There is a story about a rejected lover who promised a large sum of money to his cruel mistress's maid to be able to have the opportunity to give his mistress one last kiss during her daily walk in the bazaar. When the mistress finally gave in, he wrapped his arms around her, held her tightly, and pressed his lips so violently to her neck that an enormous violet bruise was left, with which she was forced to face her husband.

I think the Vessel, that with fugitive
Articulation answer'd, once did live
And drink; and that impassive Lip I kiss'd
How many kisses might it take—and give!

Omar Khayyam

Saw the Lesbians
kissing across their
smitten
Lutes with lips more
sweet than the sound of
lutestrings,
Mouth to mouth and
hand upon hand,
her chosen,
Fairer than all men;

Only saw the beautiful
lips and fingers,
Full of songs and kisses
and little whispers,
Full of music; only
beheld among them
Soar, as a bird soars…

Algernon Charles
Swinburne

*Daring to
mix love in those
cruel moments, his
mouth fastens to
mine and wants to
breathe the sighs
that sadness rip from
me...My tears flow,
he devours them,
alternately he kisses,
threatens, but
he continues to
hit me.*

Marquis de Sade

My lips glow with desire,
From you just one favor to acquire,
To feel your lips and to yearn
When the embers of your heart and
of your life are burning.
When this morning brought light to my eyes,
I could remember only one thought on waking,
To sink back into the grave of silken dreams,
Which eternally want you so close.
I am the slave of your kisses, which brighten
the night, kisses, in which I could melt forever.

M.S.

"As she slept, her head on my arm, I leaned over to look at her face, which was surrounded by flames. I was playing with fire. One day, as I approached too close, though our faces were not touching, I was suddenly like the needle which, having once moved a fraction of an inch beyond the mark, is in the magnet's power. Is it the fault of the magnet or the needle? I became aware that my lips were on hers. Her eyes were still closed, but she was quite obviously not asleep. I kissed her, amazed at my boldness, whereas in fact it was she who had drawn my head towards her mouth. Her hands clung to my neck; they would not have held me so fast in a shipwreck. And I did not understand whether she wanted me to save her or to drown with her."

Raymond Radiguet

The Metamorphoses of a Vampire

Meanwhile the woman, from her strawberry lips,
(Like a snake on redhot coals, writhing her hips
And working her breasts against the stays of her busk)
Let flow these words, with a heavy scent of musk:
"My mouth is wet; and I know deep in my bed
How to bury old conscience till he's dead.
On these proud breasts I wipe all tears away
And old men laugh like children at their play.
For the man who sees me naked, I replace
The moon, the sun, and all the stars of space!
And I am so expert in voluptuous charms
That when I hush a man in my terrible arms
Yielding my bosom to his biting lust,
(Shy but provocative, frail and yet robust)
The mattress swoons in commotion under me,
And the helpless angels would be damned for me!"

When she had sucked the marrow from every bone,
I turned to her as languid as a stone
To give her one last kiss…and saw her thus:
A slimy rotten wineskin, full of pus!
I shut my eyes, transfixed in a chill of fright,
And when I opened them to the living light…
Beside me there, that powerful robot
That fed its fill out of my blood…was not!
Instead, the cold ruins of a skeleton
Shivered, creaking like a weather vane
Or like a sign hung out on an iron arm
Swinging through long winter nights in the storm.

Charles Baudelaire

The warmth of our two bodies
in mixing
burns hotter
than our kisses.
Today I feel the cold
for my body
is nothing more than an icy stone
without your enchanting lips.

M.S.

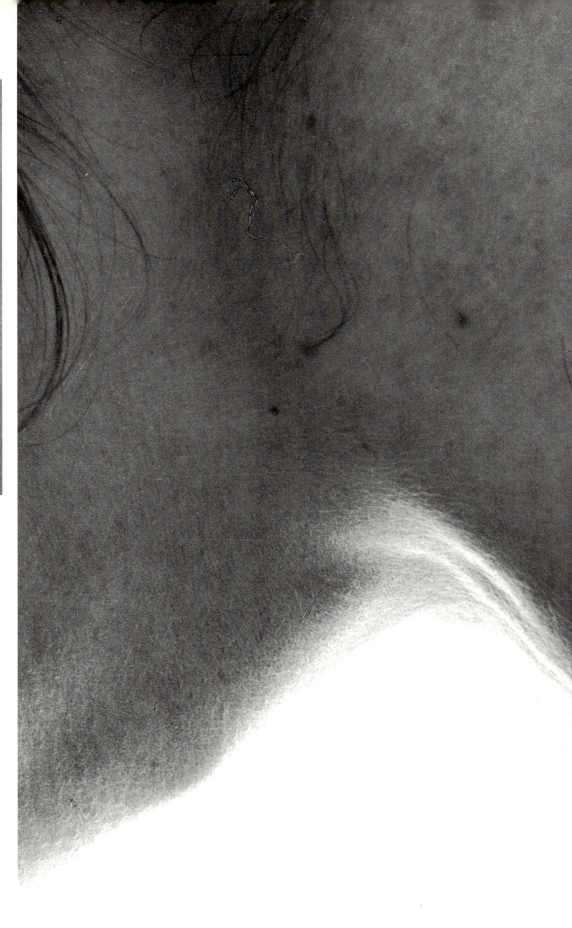

...and then I asked him
with my eyes to ask again yes and
then he asked me would I yes
to say yes and drew him down to me
so he could feel my breasts all
perfume yes and his heart
was going like mad and yes I said
yes I will Yes.

James Joyce

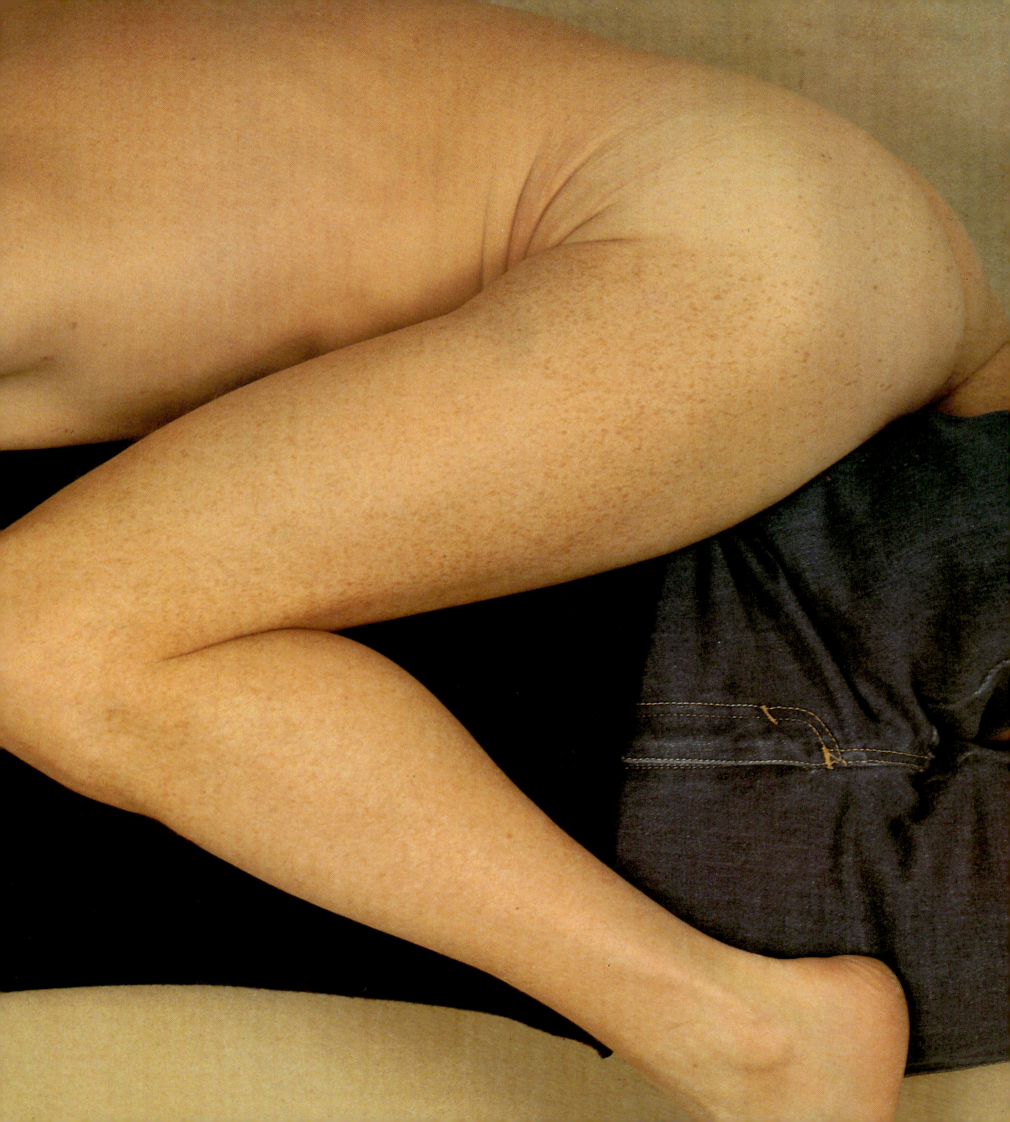

Epilogue

"Afsaneh"

The park was not too far from our house. Every afternoon we took a long walk through the marvelous alleyways and always ran into the same people on their daily outing. In this paradise of childhood I knew every tree, every bend of the way, every bench, and every stone. This is my first memory and it has carved itself deep into my heart.

"Afsaneh, you're still standing in front of that statue? Come on, let's run a little before we have to go back home," my mother said in a loud voice. It was probably the fourth time she had repeated the same sentence. It often happened that I was lost in deep reverie. I was a little dreamer—in Persian, "Afsaneh" means fairy tale. Perhaps the name had an influence on my inner life. Here I was again standing before my darling as if rooted to the ground.

There was only one statue in the whole park that always attracted my attention. When I came close to it, a magnetic force seemed to hold me before it...I could hear nothing that was going on around me and saw only the face of my chosen one. It was a young boy with prominent cheek bones, a high forehead, and almond-shaped eyes. He was life-size, hewn of a noble stone, clad in very simple clothes. He stood on the earth with one foot poised on a little platform. He rested one arm on his bent knee, and the other followed the contours of his body. He stood there in a pose that was both very merry and yet calm. He looked as if he were right there with us. His shape and proportions were so perfectly human that he seemed to mingle with us humans as if he were one of us.

The years passed and before long I was a teenager. The stone figure aroused love and passion within me, awakening desire. I dreamed of pressing my lips to his and seeing my yearning for my first kiss fulfilled.

From the very first time I recorded him in my memory, there had been a sort of silent understanding between us. He knew so much about me. He had watched me grow up and become a young woman. He belonged to the hidden world of my innermost wishes, to the innocent laugher and tears of childhood.

One day, when I was all alone taking a walk, I resolved to get very close to him and touch him. A fire burned in me and my heart beat wildly. How would he react to our first face-to-face meeting?

I found him more radiant than ever. I laid my

hand on his and felt an unbelievable softness, a delicious fragility. He was not cold the way stone normally is. He exuded a warmth which made me blush. A tremendous force suddenly compelled me to his breast as though a storm had swept me there. And then my lips touched his. I stole the long-desired kiss from him! And in that instant he began to mumur indecipherable words, and his voice sounded as though it were awakening from a hundred-year sleep. He made great efforts to tell me an eternal secret, and I did not move from where I was standing. I stood glued to the spot, very close to him. I heard him as though from far away, from the depth of his heart: "Every part of my body that you touch with your lips will awaken. Your kiss brings me life. This mouth, overflowing with love and tenderness, gives me the strength to return to life and tell you that I love you."

Tears streamed down my face as I listened to his words. With a strong voice he continued: "Kiss my eyes so that I may see you and tell you how beautiful you are!"

I kissed his eyes and immediately they flew open. His innocent gaze touched me and enveloped me in its magic. He said: "Kiss my hands so that I may feel the softness of your skin and the warmth of your body." I followed all his instructions like a robot drunk with love for its master.

I experienced a dream in a faraway kingdom in which I could have stayed forever. And had time stood still at that moment, I would have achieved eternal bliss! His voice was very clear and overwhelmed me with sentences that sent me into ecstasy: "Don't leave me; I cannot live without you, without your generous love. I have spent my whole life watching others live and now it is my turn to be loved and passionately desired. For lack of love I became a statue, because I couldn't live without it. Once you have experienced love, you can never live without it and you await only the day when it will return. This day has come...Your love is the blood flowing through my veins and without it I am only a cold, soulless statue."

This confession moved me, awoke in me the desire to love and be loved. Still, mingled with my desire and longing was a feeling of fear, because I also began to imagine the deep responsibility that love demands. In reality, I didn't know love myself but simply allowed its force to lead me.

Then I began to cover the boy from head to toe with kisses—his whole body and also his heart. And with every kiss the power of life flowed into him. Suddenly he took his first step and together we went away, very far from reality.

Appendix
Illustration Credits

(Cover, p.2) © Helmut Newton

(p.6) © David Hamilton, Private estate

(p.8) © Rainer Leitzgen, Munich

(p.18) © Henri Cartier-Bresson, Magnum

(pp.26-7) André Kertész, Lovers, Budapest, May 15, 1915; © Estate of André Kertész, New York

(p.27) Brassaï, Lovers in a Small Parisian Café, c. 1932; © Gilberte Brassaï

(pp.28-9) Robert Doisneau, Kiss in Front of the City Hall; © Doisneau-Rapho, Paris

(pp.30-1) Robert Doisneau, Box; © Doisneau-Rapho, Paris

(p.31) A Couple in a Café; © H. Roger-Viollet, Paris

(pp.32-3) Brooklyn, New York; © Bruce Davidson, Magnum

(p.34) Erich Salomon, Carnival Mood, 1929; © Berlin Gallery, Erich Salomon Archives, Image archive of the Prussian Cultural Estate, Berlin

(p.35) Alfred Eisenstadt, 1945, Life Magazine; © Time Warner Inc., New York

(p.36) Dieppe, 1926; © Henri Cartier-Bresson, Magnum

(pp.36-7) © Patrick Zachmann, Magnum

(p.38) New York City, 1981; © 1989 Mandy Vahabzadeh

(p.39) Farewell Kiss for the Boys; © UPI/Bettmann Newsphotos, New York

(p.40) Brassaï, Lovers; © Gilberte Brassaï

(pp.40-1) © Elliott Erwitt, Magnum

(p.42) Central Park, New York, 1977; © Vincent Mentzel, Art Unlimited, Amsterdam

(pp.44-5) Café de Flore, 1958, Paris; © Dennis Stock, Magnum

(p.43) New Orleans, 1988; © Franco Zecchin, Magnum

(p.46) Maryam Sachs With Her Daughter Roya; © Thomas Zwink, Munich

(pp.50-1) The First Kiss for the Little Brother; © Jan Saudek, Art Unlimited, Amsterdam

(p.52) © Jan Saudek, Art Unlimited, Amsterdam

(p.53) © Jan Saudek, Art Unlimited, Amsterdam

(p.54) © Trevor Watson, Portfolio Gallery, London

(p.55) © Jan Saudek, Art Unlimited, Amsterdam

(pp.56-7) Hans Staub, In Front of the Day Care Center in the Industrial Zone, Zurich, 1931; © Stiftung für die Photographie, Art House Zurich

(p.57) © Woodfin Camp & Associates, Inc., New York

(p.60) © The Image Bank, Munich

191

(p.58) © Prof. Robert Häusser, Mannheim

(p.61) © Werner Sittig, Edermünde

(p.62) © Fernando Baptista, Art Unlimited, Amsterdam

(p.63) © Flashcards, Inc., West Oakland

(p.64) © Flashcards, Inc., West Oakland

(p.65) © The Image Bank, Munich

(pp.66) © Helga Lade Photo Agency, Frankfurt/Main

(pp.66-7) © Mike Hollist, Art Unlimited, Amsterdam

(pp.68-9) Marc Paygnard, The Kiss, 1979; © Rapho, Paris

(p.70) © Phil Stern Photo, Los Angeles

(p.71) © Amadeus, IFA-Image team, Taufkirchen

(p.72) © Hans Madej, Bilderberg, Hamburg

(pp.72-3) At the Moscow Circus; © V. Yatsina, Sovfoto, New York

(p.74) L.A. Model Advertising Campaign; © Ross Whitaker, New York

(p.77) © Musée Carnavalet, Photographie Bulloz, Paris

(p.78) © Jean Dubout, Paris

(p.80) © ND-Viollet, Paris

(p.81) © H. Roger-Viollet, Paris

(pp.82-3) Collage; © Rolf Sachs, Munich

(pp.84-5) Just Married, 1986; © Gert Weigelt, Art Unlimited, Amsterdam

(pp.86-7) George Karger, © Life Magazine, Time Warner Inc., New York

(pp.88-9) © Pete Turner, New York

(p.87) © 1990 Allan Grant, Allan Grant Productions, Los Angeles

(p.90) © dpa/epa, Munich

(p.92) Pope John Paul II in Santo Domingo, 1979; © dpa, Munich

(p.97) The Duke and Duchess of Windsor; © UPI/Bettmann Newsphotos, New York

(p.96) Grace Kelly and Prince Rainier of Monaco at a Gala in the Waldorf Astoria Hotel in New York— One Day After Announcing Their Engagement; © 1956 Pictorial Parade, Inc., New York

(p.98) Boris Becker Wins Wimbledon in 1985; © Rüdiger Schrader, dpa, Munich

(p.99) Björn Borg, Wimbledon 1979; © Image Department of the Süddeutscher Verlag, Munich

(pp.100-1) Kiss on the Hand for Jacqueline Kennedy, 1963; © UPI/Bettmann Newsphotos, New York

(p.102) Homage to the Shah, Isfahan, Iran 1963; © *Thomas Höpker, Anne Hamann Agency, Munich*

(p.103) Pablo Picasso with Jacqueline Roque, 1961; © *Pictorial Parade, New York*

(pp.104-5) Andy Warhol Exchanging Feigned Proofs of Warmth and Tenderness with Liza Minelli, John Lennon, Salvador Dalí and Philipp Johnson; © *Christopher Makos, New York*

(p.109) George Bush giving a conventional kiss to a nun; © *Mike Barber/Suburban News Publications, Columbus, Ohio*

(p.106) During the Oscar Award Ceremony in Hollywood in 1985 Michael Douglas kisses his father, Kirk Douglas; © *dpa/epa, Munich*

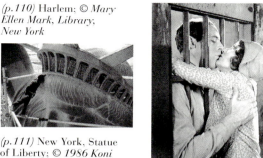

(p.107) Mikhail Baryshnikov with the dancers of the American Ballet Theatre (from left to right) Careen Hobart, Julie Kent, and Elizabeth Dunn; © *1990, Annie Leibovitz, Contact Press, Focus, Hamburg*

(pp.108-9) Mikhail Gorbachev giving the Socialist brotherly kiss to Erich Honecker, 1987; © *dpa, Munich*

(p.110) Harlem; © *Mary Ellen Mark, Library, New York*

(p.111) New York, Statue of Liberty; © *1986 Koni Nordmann, Contact Press Images*

(p.112) Marilyn Monroe; © *UPI/Bettmann Newsphotos, New York*

(p.114) The first kiss in a movie caused a scandal in New York in 1896. It was the kiss exchanged between May Irvin and John Rice in the movie "The Kiss" by Graff and Gammon, based on the play "The Widow Jones"; © *Cinestar*

(p.115) © *Walt Disney Productions*

(pp.116-7) Ruhr District, Drive-in Theater; © *Milan Horacek, Bilderberg, Hamburg*

(p.118) Scene from "Hell's Island"; © *Culver Pictures, New York*

(p.119) Jean Gabin kisses Geneviève Tubin; © *Culver Pictures, New York*

(p.120-1) Scene from "Seven Days," with Lillian Rich, Creighton Hale, Lilyan Tashman, Eddie Gribbon, Mabel Julienne Scott, and Hallam Cooley; © *Culver Pictures, New York*

(p.123) Victor McLaglen, Greta Nissen, and Edmund Lowe in "Women of All Nations" directed by Raoul Walsh; © *Culver Pictures, New York*

(p.122) Constance Talmadge seducing her victim Ronald Colman in "Her Sister from Paris" produced by Joseph M. Schenck; © *Culver Pictures, New York*

(p.124) Alla Nazimova and Rudolph Valentino; © *Motion Picture and Television Photo Archive, Los Angeles*

(p.125) Cary Grant and Grace Kelly in "To Catch a Thief"; © *Image Archive Peter Engelmeier, Munich*

(pp.126-7) Rosalind Russell and James Stewart (first row, center) invited a hundred engaged couples to the premiere of their radio play "First Love." Here they instructed their guests of honor in the correct kissing technique for a close-up; © *Everett Collection, New York*

(p.127) Marilyn Monroe and Sir Lawrence Olivier in the enchanting erotic comedy "The Prince and the Show Girl," 1957; © *Photofest, New York*

(p.128) Jean Harlow and Clark Gable in the movie "Red Dust," 1932; © *Culver Pictures, New York*

(p.129) Vivien Leigh and Clark Gable in "Gone with the Wind," 1939. This is probably the most famous kiss in movie history; © *Pictorial Parade, New York*

(pp.130-1) Greta Garbo and John Gilbert in "Flesh and the Devil," 1927; © *Image Archive Peter Engelmeier, Munich*

(p.132) Maurice Chevalier and Jeanette MacDonald in "The Merry Widow." 1934; © Photofest, New York

(p.136) Cary Grant and Ingrid Bergman in "Notorious." 1948; © Collection Télérama, Editions Zreik, Paris

(p.140) Roy Lichtenstein, The Kiss. 1964, oil and magma on canvas, Two panels, 68 x 24" and 68 x 68"; © VAGA, New York

(p.148) René Lalique, Pendant, gold, rock crystal, enamel 4.7 x 5.9 cm; © Fundaçao Calouste Gulbenkian-Museu, Lisbon

(p.152) © Julian Schnabel, The Kiss. 1988, oil and plaster on canvas, 16' x 16'

(p.157) Franz von Stuck, Muggy Night, Private estate

(p.133) Lauren Bacall and Humphrey Bogart in "To Have and Have Not." 1944; © Image Department of the Süddeutscher Verlag, Munich

(pp.136-7) Cary Grant and Ingrid Bergman in "Notorious." 1948; © The Kobal Collection, London

(p.145) Gustav Klimt, The Kiss; 1908, © Archive for Art and History, Berlin

(p.149) René Lalique, Pendant brooch, ivory, enamel 7.2 x 7.2 cm; © Fundaçao Calouste Gulbenkian-Museu, Lisbon

(pp.138-9) Elizabeth Taylor and Richard Burton in the gangster movie "The Comedians." 1967; © Central Press, Pictorial Parade, Inc., New York

(p.146) Edvard Munch, The Kiss, 1902, wood engraving; © Oslo Kommunes Kunstsamlinger Munch-Museet, Oslo

(p.150) Giotto, Judas' Kiss. fresco, Padua, Scrovegni Chapel; © Archive for Art and History, Berlin

(p.153) Agnolo Bronzino, 1503–1572, Allegoria, oil on wood, 146 x 116 cm, London, National Gallery; © Archive for Art and History, Berlin

(pp.154-5) Jean-Honoré Fragonard, The Stolen Kiss. 1766; © The Hermitage Museum, Leningrad

(p.159) Robert Longo, Strong in Love, 1983, acrylic, pencil, and graphite on canvas 165 x 395 cm; © Gallerie Bernd Klüser, Munich

(p.134) Alexander Gray and Bernice Claire in "Song of the Flame," 1930; © Culver Pictures, New York

(p.139) Drew Barrymore kisses E.T. in Steven Spielberg's "E.T. The Extraterrestrial," 1982; © Pictorial Parade, Inc., New York

(p.147) Peter Behrens, The Kiss, 1900, color wood engraving; © Artothek, Peissenberg

(p.156) Pablo Picasso, Two Figures with a Cat, 1902, watercolor and pastel, 18 x 26.5 cm; © Museu Picasso, Barcelona

(pp.160-1) Auguste Rodin, Eternal Spring, 1884; © Photographie Bulloz, Paris

(p.135) Mary Duncan and Antonio Moreno in "Romance of the Rio Grande." 1929; © Culver Pictures, New York

(p.144) Henri de Toulouse-Lautrec, The Kiss on the Bed; © Photographie Bulloz, Paris

(p.151) Francesco Hayez, The Kiss, 1859, oil on canvas, 119 x 88 cm; © Archive for Art and History, Berlin

(p.161) Camille Claudel, Sakountala, 1888; © Photographie Bulloz, Paris

(p.162) © Kishin Shinoyana, Tokyo

(p.164) Maraini, Cloth from a Tibetan Temple, nineteenth century; Collezione Fosco; © Scala, Antella/Florence

(p.166) © Gunter Sachs

(p.167) © Gunter Sachs

(pp.170-2) © Werner Pavlok, Stuttgart, Private estate

(pp.173-5) © Werner Pavlok, Stuttgart, Private estate

(p.169) © Werner Pavlok, Stuttgart, Private estate

(p.168) Pedro Uhart, Dracula Kiss; © Comptoir de la Photographie, Paris

(p.178) © Helmut Newton

(p.179) © Helmut Newton

(pp.180-1) © Helmut Newton

(pp.176-7) © Rainer Leitzgen, Munich

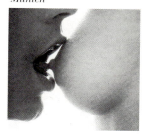

(p.182) © Bernd Schaier, Munich

(p.183) © Bernd Schaier, Munich

(p.184) © Will McBride/G.P.A., Munich

(pp.184-5) © Will McBride/G.P.A., Munich

(pp.186-7) John Lennon and Yoko Ono, several hours before his murder; © 1980, Annie Leibovitz, Focus, Hamburg

Bibliography

Alighieri, Dante. *The Divine Comedy of Dante Alighieri, Inferno.* Trans. John D. Sinclair. New York: Oxford University Press, 1972.

Amad, Gladys. *Le Baiser Rituel.* Beirut: 1973.

Bartlett, John. *Bartlett's Familiar Quotations.* Boston: Little, Brown and Company, 1980.

Barthes, Roland. *A Lover's Discourse: Fragments.* New York: Howard, Hill and Wang, 1978.

Baudelaire, Charles. *The Flowers of Evil.* Trans. Jackson Mathews. New York: New Directions, 1963.

Bazin, Hervé. *Abécédaire, Discours sur la Bouche.* Paris: 1984.

Bécquer, Gustavo Adolfo. *Rimas y Leyendas.* Madrid: 1979.

Bédier, Joseph. *Roman de Tristan et Iseult.* Paris: 1941.

Belleau, Rémy. *La Bergerie.* Geneva: 1954.

Bonaparte, Napoleon. *Briefe an Josephine.* Munich: 1967.

Der neue Brockhaus. Wiesbaden: 1985.

Casanova, Giacomo. *Memoiren.* Hamburg: 1966.

Catullus, Gaius Valerius. *Selected Translations 1948–1968.* Trans. W. S. Merwin. New York: Atheneum, 1968.

Chekhov, Anton. *The Portable Chekhov.* New York: Viking Press, 1968.

Cohen, J. M. and M. J. Cohen, eds. *The Penguin Dictionary of Quotations:* London: 1960.

Cohen, J.M. and M.J. Cohen, eds. *The Penguin Dictionary of Quotations.* London: Allen Lane/Penguin Books Ltd., 1977.

Colette. *The Ripening Seed.* Trans. Roger Senhouse. New York: Farrar, Strauss & Giroux, 1955.

Colette. *The Vagabond.* Trans. Enid McLeod. New York: Farrar, Strauss & Giroux, 1955.

Comarnescu, Peter. *Brancusi.* Paris: Arted Editions d'Art, 1982.

Cotton, Charles. *Poems on Several Occasions.* London: 1689.

d'Enjoy, Paul. "Le Baiser en Europe et en Chine." *Bulletin de la Société d'Anthropologie de Paris,* April 1,1897.

Dictionary of Christian Antiquity and Liturgy

Dictionary of Osculation. England: 1873.

Dictionnaire de Trévoux, Dictionnaire Universal Français et Latin, Nouvelle édition. Paris: Compagnie des libraires associés, 1771.

Dictionnaire des Citations Françaises et Etrangères. Paris: 1980.

Dubout, Jean. *Kama Soutra.* Paris: 1979.

Duden. *Deutsches Universalwörterbuch.* Wien/Zürich: 1989.

Éluard, Paul. *Letters to Gala.* Trans. Jesse Browner. New York: Paragon House, 1989.

Fasquelle, Eugène. *Le Livre des Mille et une Nuits.* Paris: 1905.

Fauche, Xavier and Christiane Noetzlin. *Le Baiser.* Paris: 1987.

Fielding, Henry. *The History of the Adventures of Joseph Andrews.* Munich: 1965.

Frank, Ann. *Tagebuch der Ann Frank.* Frankfurt: 1955.

Franklin, Alfred. "La Loterie d'Amour." *La Vie Privée d'Autrefois,* Plou; 1887.

Fraser, Antonia. *Love Letters.* London: 1976.

Freud, Sigmund. *Studienausgabe,* Volume V: *Sexualleben.* Frankfurt: 1972.

Freud, Sigmund. *Drei Abhandlungen zur Sexualtheorie.* Leipzig/Wien: 1926.

Garrigue, Jean, ed. *Love's Aspects: The World's Great Love Poems.* New York: Doubleday & Company, 1975.

Geist, Sidney. *Brancusi, The Kiss.* New York: Harper & Row, 1978.

Goethe, Johann Wolfgang von. *Werke, Hamburg ed.: Faust, Part 1.* Munich: 1981.

Goethe, Johann Wolfgang von. *Goethes Werke, Hamburg ed.: Romane und Novellen I.* Munich: 1981.

The Golden Tradition: An Anthology of Urdu Poetry. Columbia University Press, 1973.

Gourmont, Rémy de. In Emile Malespine, "The Kiss," *Le Forum* (July, 1921).

Grigson, Geoffrey, ed. *The Faber Book of Love Poems.* London: 1973.

Grigson, Geoffrey, ed. *The Gambit Book of Love Poems.* Boston: Gambit, 1975.

Grimm, Brüder. *Deutsches Wörterbuch, Band 5.* Deutscher Taschenbuchverlag. Munich: 1984.

Hastings, James, ed. *Encyclopedia of Religion and Ethics.* New York: Charles Scribner's Sons, 1915.

Haton, René. *Notice sur les Instruments de Paix.* Paris: 1865.

Hebdo Magazine. Paris: April 1, 1932.

Heine, Heinrich. *Buch der Lieder.* Munich: 1987.

Heine, Heinrich. *Gedichte.* Munich: 1969.

Hemingway, Ernest. *For Whom the Bell Tolls.* New York: Charles Scribner's Sons, 1968.

Herbermann, Charles, ed. *The Catholic Encyclopedia.* New York: Robert Appleton Company, 1910.

Herodotus. *Historien,* Volume 1. Munich: 1963.

Herrick, Robert. *Selections from The Hesperides and Noble Numbers of Robert Herrick*, New York: Harper & Brothers, 1882.

Hesse, Hermann. *Siddhartha*. Trans. Hilda Rosner. New York: New Directions, 1951.

Homer. *The Iliad*. Munich: 1957.

Homer. *The Odyssey*. Munich: 1957.

Hugo, Victor. *Die Elenden*. Munich: 1963.

Joyce, James. *The Portable James Joyce*. Ed. Harry Levin. Viking Press, 1966.

Kafka, Franz. *Gesammelte Werke, Briefe an Felice*. Frankfurt: 1967.

Khayyam, Omar. *Die Rubaijat des Omar Khayyam*. Frankfurt: 1963.

Kinsey, Alfred Charles. *Sexual Behavior in the Human Male*. Philadelphia: W.B. Saunders Company, 1948.

"The Kiss Poetical." *Fortnightly Review* LXXXII (August 1904).

Labé, Louise. *Love Sonnets*. Trans. Frederic Prokosch. New York: New Directions, 1947.

Laclos, Choderlos de. *Les Liaisons Dangereuses*. Paris: 1782.

Lahr, Jane and Lena Tabori. *Love, A Celebration in Art and Literature*. New York: Stewart, Tabori & Chang, 1982.

Lambron, Marc. *L'Impromptu de Madrid*. Paris: 1988

Lombroso, Cesare. "L'Origine du Baiser." *La Nouvelle Revue*. Paris.

Longus. *Daphnis und Chloë*. Berlin: 1980.

Malespine, Emile. "The Kiss." *Le Forum*, LXVI (July 1921).

Martial. *Römischer Witz*. Munich: 1960.

Maupassant, Guy de. *Romane, Ein Leben*. Munich: 1974.

Mehta, Rustam Jahangu. *The Love-Kiss in the East and the West, Kama-Chumbana*, Washington: 1969.

Méry, Fernand. *Bêtes et Gens devant l'Amour*. Paris: 1952.

Mirbeau, Octave. *Tagebuch einer Zofe*. Munich: 1967.

Morin, Edgard. *Les Stars*. Paris: 1972.

Morris, Desmond. *Bodywatching*. New York: Crown Publishers, Inc., 1985.

Mourier, Martine and Jean-Luc Tournier. *La Petite Encyclopédie du Baiser*. Ed. Pierre-Marcel Favre. Lausanne: 1984.

Nézami. *Leili and Majnoun*. London: 1836.

Nourissier, François. *Le corps de Diane*. Paris: 1957.

Nyrop, Christopher. *The Kiss and Its History*. Michigan: Singing Tree Press, 1968.

Ovid. *The Art of Love*. Trans. J. H. Mozley. Cambridge: Harvard University Press, 1962.

Oxford English Dictionary. Oxford: Clarendon Press.

Perella, Nicolas James. *The Kiss Sacred and Profane*. Berkeley and Los Angeles: University of California Press, 1969.

Pound, Ezra. *Translations*. New York: New Directions, 1963.

Prévert, Jacques. *Blood and Feathers; Selected Poems of Jacques Prévert*. Trans. Harriet Zinnes. New York: Schocken Books, 1988.

Proust, Marcel. *Remembrance of Things Past*, Volume 1. Trans. C.K. Scott Moncrieff. Random House.

Radiguet, Raymond. *The Devil in the Flesh*. Trans. A. M. Sheridan Smith. London: Marion Boyers Publishers, 1982.

Reboux, Paul. *Die neue Lebensart*. Munich: 1932.

Reboux, Paul. *Pour Balayer les Vieux Usages, Voici le Nouveau Savoir-Vivre*, Paris: 1965.

Renard, Jules. *Journal 1887-1910*. Paris: 1990.

Ronsard, Pierre de. *Sonette der Liebe*. Mainz: 1948.

Rostand, Edmond. *Cyrano de Bergerac*. Trans. Anthony Burgess. Vintage Books, 1990.

Schiller, Friedrich von. *Die Räuber*. 1781.

Schiller, Friedrich von. *Poems 1777–1805 in Two Volumes*.

Shah Zafar, Bahdur Ahmed Ali. *Die Goldene Tradition*. New York/London: 1973.

Shakespeare, William. *Complete Works*. Oxford: Oxford University Press, 1986.

Singer, Isodore, ed. *The Jewish Encyclopedia*. New York: Funk and Wagnalls Company, 1904.

Stendhal. *Das Leben des Henry Brulard und autobiografische Schriften*. Munich: 1956.

Süskind, Patrick. *Das Parfum*. Zürich: 1985.

Tristan and Isolde. Leipzig: 1911.

Truffaut, François. *Hitchcock*. New York: Simon & Schuster, 1983.

Vadim, Roger. *Bardot Deneuve Fonda*. Trans. Melinda Camber Porter. New York: Simon & Schuster, 1986.

Vadim, Roger. *D'une Étiole à l'Autre*. Paris: 1986.

"Valentins et Valentines." *Annales du Musée Guimet, in Revue de l'Histoire des Religions*, Paris (1985).

van Gulik, Robert. *La Vie Sexuelle dans la Chine Ancienne*. Paris: 1977.

Vatsyayana, Mallanaga. *Kamasutram*. Berlin: 1915.

Verlaine, Paul. *Les Femmes*. Trans. Alistair Elliot. London: Anvil Press Poetry, 1979.

Webster's New World Dictionary of Quotable Definitions. New York: 1970.

Wilde, Oscar. *Die Ballade vom Zuchthaus zu Reading*. Leipzig: 1970.

The author and the publisher wish to thank
the many publishing houses for their support and for
the permission to reprint the excerpted texts.

I owe special thanks to Rolf Heyne, who
supported my idea for this book.
I also wish to thank Hans-Peter Übleis for
his diplomatic talents.
I owe much to Christian Diener, who
inspired me time and again and passed along
some excellent artistic ideas.
I am very grateful to Ria Lottermoser for her
tireless efforts and her commitment to this project.
I would also like to thank Paul Fugmann for
consultation on technical questions.
I would also like to gratefully mention those who
contributed at a distance: Katsuyo Motoyoshi,
Bijan Aalam, Marc Lambron, and
Dr. Wolfgang Reinicke.
I would like to thank the photographers and painters
who loaned me their works: David Hamilton,
Julian Schnabel, Werner Pawlok,
and my father-in-law Gunter Sachs.
I thank Monica Eckert, Manfred Erber,
and Frank Burger for their readiness to give
me their time and knowledge.
I profusely thank Sheytoun, who supported
me with all his heart.
My greatest gratitude to my parents,
without whom I would not be here in the first place.
And a special message to Philipp, Frederik, and
Roya, who gave me strength. To them
go my most tender kisses.